Who The F*ck Am I?!

77 Questions To Help You Gain Greater Self Awareness

by

ERIK MYERS

SOCIAL MEDIA

Instagram

@erkmurs
@erikmyers4

GET IN TOUCH

erikmyers1991@gmail.com

Created by Erik Myers

ISBN 9798662703841

The Inevitable Question

If you are a human being living on planet Earth, at one point or on a daily basis, you ask yourself, "Who the fuck am I?". Maybe you don't cuss like a sailor (or maybe you do since you and your twisted mind picked up this book) but that curiosity of our own true nature can and will keep the best of us up late at night.

While some people know themselves from an early age and gracefully swift through life, the far majority of us are left haunted by our own uncertainty. I know because I, too, have spent far too much time wondering who I am and why I'm here.

For most of my 20's, I've been reading books and watching videos designed to help develop a stronger sense of self-awareness and what I've learned has been pretty disappointing. It's incredibly difficult to accomplish this feat when we're receiving the answers and advice from an external source, often leaving us with more questions than answers.

Instead, I've come to my best conclusions when I'm drawing the answers from internal exploration. That simple realization is what led to the creation of this journal in your hands. I've compiled a list of 77 questions that have helped me better understand myself over the years and I'm hopeful that they can help you do the same. How you use this journal is completely up to you.

You can answer one question a day, you can take off for a weekend getaway where you deep dive and fill them all out, or you can pick and choose which questions you're curious in dissecting and skip the rest. Your answers can be short and sweet or you can fill out the entire page. As Kevin Hart would say, "Do you, Boo Boo."

Only **you** know how it will be best utilized and applied to your life.

I do have one recommendation. Please be 100% brutally-fuckin'-honest with yourself and your answers. No one needs to read them and you'll be selling yourself short if you don't keep it real.

By the time you're done with this journal, my hope is that your internal dialogue is transitioning from "Who the fuck am I?" to "I know who the fuck I am" and you begin to trust your instincts, which will lead to daily decision-making that reflects your true self and desires.

Self-awareness is not a task to check off your to-do list, it's a lifelong exploration that's constantly evolving. The more you align yourself with that flow, the smoother your ride will be. But it must be bumpy before it smoothes out and these questions will guide you to the other side.

Now buckle up and let's get to work.

1. What area(s) of your life are you crushing it?

_____

_____

_____

_____

_____

_____

_____

_____

_____

_____

_____

_____

_____

_____

_____

_____

2. What area(s) of your life do you need to do better?

_____

_____

_____

_____

_____

_____

_____

_____

_____

_____

_____

_____

_____

_____

_____

3. What's a skill or hobby that you've always wanted to learn, but always put off?

_____

_____

_____

_____

_____

_____

_____

_____

_____

_____

_____

_____

_____

_____

_____

4. What activities are you doing when you lose track of time because you're completely immersed in the moment and engaged in the task?

_____

_____

_____

_____

_____

_____

_____

_____

_____

_____

_____

_____

_____

_____

_____

5. If you were being the best version of yourself, what would that look and feel like?

_____

_____

_____

_____

_____

_____

_____

_____

_____

_____

_____

_____

_____

_____

6. When you're in pain, what do you do to feel better?

_____

_____

_____

_____

_____

_____

_____

_____

_____

_____

_____

_____

_____

_____

7. What does happiness mean to you?

_____

_____

_____

_____

_____

_____

_____

_____

_____

_____

_____

_____

_____

_____

_____

8. What's one thing that you can live without?

_____

_____

_____

_____

_____

_____

_____

_____

_____

_____

_____

_____

_____

_____

_____

9. What's one thing that you can't live without?

_____

_____

_____

_____

_____

_____

_____

_____

_____

_____

_____

_____

_____

_____

10. Do you believe all the thoughts that cross through your mind? And which thoughts about yourself do you believe in and repeat the most?

_____

_____

_____

_____

_____

_____

_____

_____

_____

_____

_____

_____

_____

11. If money were irrelevant- what would you love to be doing 8 hours a day, 40 hours a week?

_____

_____

_____

_____

_____

_____

_____

_____

_____

_____

_____

_____

_____

_____

12. Who brings out the best in you? Who is the person, or people, who make you feel the most comfortable to be yourself?

_____

_____

_____

_____

_____

_____

_____

_____

_____

_____

_____

_____

_____

_____

13. Who drains your energy? Who do you feel like you have to hide your true self around?

_____

_____

_____

_____

_____

_____

_____

_____

_____

_____

_____

_____

_____

_____

_____

14. **What's the best advice you've ever received that you consistently implement?**

_____

_____

_____

_____

_____

_____

_____

_____

_____

_____

_____

_____

_____

_____

15.   Where do you go when you need to calm and center yourself?

_____

_____

_____

_____

_____

_____

_____

_____

_____

_____

_____

_____

_____

_____

16. What is your biggest fear? And if it were to happen, what would you do?

_____

_____

_____

_____

_____

_____

_____

_____

_____

_____

_____

_____

_____

_____

17. **Do you get your energy from being by yourself or when you're surrounded by others?**

_____

_____

_____

_____

_____

_____

_____

_____

_____

_____

_____

_____

_____

_____

18. **What part of the day do you feel the most creative?**

_____

_____

_____

_____

_____

_____

_____

_____

_____

_____

_____

_____

_____

_____

19. **What would you like to be remembered for?**

_____

_____

_____

_____

_____

_____

_____

_____

_____

_____

_____

_____

_____

_____

20. What do you love learning about?

_____

_____

_____

_____

_____

_____

_____

_____

_____

_____

_____

_____

_____

_____

21. What's something from your past that you've haven't been able to let go of?

_____

_____

_____

_____

_____

_____

_____

_____

_____

_____

_____

_____

_____

_____

22. What does success mean to you?

_____

_____

_____

_____

_____

_____

_____

_____

_____

_____

_____

_____

_____

_____

_____

23.   How do you want to be viewed by others?

_____

_____

_____

_____

_____

_____

_____

_____

_____

_____

_____

_____

_____

_____

_____

24. What's your most important priority for this stage of your life?

_____

_____

_____

_____

_____

_____

_____

_____

_____

_____

_____

_____

_____

_____

25. If/when you have children, what's the most important piece of advice to give them?

_____

_____

_____

_____

_____

_____

_____

_____

_____

_____

_____

_____

_____

_____

_____

26. What is your biggest obstacle these days? And what do you need to do differently to overcome it?

_____

_____

_____

_____

_____

_____

_____

_____

_____

_____

_____

_____

_____

_____

27.   What are the four words that best describe yourself?

_____

_____

_____

_____

_____

_____

_____

_____

_____

_____

_____

_____

_____

_____

28. What quality do you admire in other people that you'd like to have?

_____

_____

_____

_____

_____

_____

_____

_____

_____

_____

_____

_____

_____

_____

29. Describe the best moment of your life. Where were you? What were you doing? How did it feel? Why is it unforgettable?

_____

_____

_____

_____

_____

_____

_____

_____

_____

_____

_____

_____

_____

30.   **What makes me the most angry? And why do I get so upset about it?**

_____

_____

_____

_____

_____

_____

_____

_____

_____

_____

_____

_____

_____

31. **What achievement are you most proud of so far in your life?**

_____

_____

_____

_____

_____

_____

_____

_____

_____

_____

_____

_____

_____

_____

32. **What achievement do you crave in your near future? Distant future?**

_____

_____

_____

_____

_____

_____

_____

_____

_____

_____

_____

_____

_____

33. What makes you the most stressed out? What about it stresses you out so much?

_____

_____

_____

_____

_____

_____

_____

_____

_____

_____

_____

_____

_____

_____

34. What do you admire about yourself?

_____

_____

_____

_____

_____

_____

_____

_____

_____

_____

_____

_____

_____

_____

35. **What is your biggest regret? What did you learn from that experience?**

_____

_____

_____

_____

_____

_____

_____

_____

_____

_____

_____

_____

_____

36. How do you spend the majority of your free time?

_____

_____

_____

_____

_____

_____

_____

_____

_____

_____

_____

_____

_____

37. How would you describe your childhood?

_____

_____

_____

_____

_____

_____

_____

_____

_____

_____

_____

_____

_____

_____

38. What worries you the most about your future? What can you do now to prepare for it?

_____

_____

_____

_____

_____

_____

_____

_____

_____

_____

_____

_____

_____

_____

39. What secret will you take to the grave with you?

_____

_____

_____

_____

_____

_____

_____

_____

_____

_____

_____

_____

_____

_____

_____

_____

40. Do you give as much as you take? In what ways can you give more?

_____

_____

_____

_____

_____

_____

_____

_____

_____

_____

_____

_____

_____

41. What do you most often take for granted? What can you do differently to appreciate it more frequently?

_____

_____

_____

_____

_____

_____

_____

_____

_____

_____

_____

_____

_____

42. Do you think negative thoughts before you go to sleep?

_____

_____

_____

_____

_____

_____

_____

_____

_____

_____

_____

_____

_____

_____

43. **If you were told you had six months to live, what would you do?**

_____

_____

_____

_____

_____

_____

_____

_____

_____

_____

_____

_____

_____

_____

44. Who has had the greatest impact on your life? What did they teach you?

_____

_____

_____

_____

_____

_____

_____

_____

_____

_____

_____

_____

_____

_____

45. If you could pursue your passion and there's no way you could fail at it, what would you do?

_____

_____

_____

_____

_____

_____

_____

_____

_____

_____

_____

_____

_____

_____

46. How much do you care about other people's opinion of you? Honestly.

_____

_____

_____

_____

_____

_____

_____

_____

_____

_____

_____

_____

_____

47. **Do you believe that you have control of your life? Or is life controlling you?**

_____

_____

_____

_____

_____

_____

_____

_____

_____

_____

_____

_____

_____

_____

48. What small part of your day consistently makes you smile? What do you love about it?

_____

_____

_____

_____

_____

_____

_____

_____

_____

_____

_____

_____

_____

49. **What's your all-time favorite quote? What does it mean to you?**

_____

_____

_____

_____

_____

_____

_____

_____

_____

_____

_____

_____

_____

_____

_____

50. Describe an "out of body" experience you've had that you'll never forget.

_____

_____

_____

_____

_____

_____

_____

_____

_____

_____

_____

_____

_____

_____

51.   **What always brings tears to your eyes?**

_____

_____

_____

_____

_____

_____

_____

_____

_____

_____

_____

_____

_____

_____

_____

52. What was your favorite class in high school/college? What did you love about it and what did you learn from it?

_____

_____

_____

_____

_____

_____

_____

_____

_____

_____

_____

_____

_____

53. Describe a time when your work felt important, necessary, and satisfying to you.

_____

_____

_____

_____

_____

_____

_____

_____

_____

_____

_____

_____

_____

_____

54. **What's surprised you the most about your life so far?**

_____

_____

_____

_____

_____

_____

_____

_____

_____

_____

_____

_____

_____

_____

55. What's a question/curiosity you have that you desperately need an answer for?

_____

_____

_____

_____

_____

_____

_____

_____

_____

_____

_____

_____

_____

_____

56. What's missing in your life? What can you do to fill it?

_____

_____

_____

_____

_____

_____

_____

_____

_____

_____

_____

_____

_____

_____

57. How is the "public you" different from the "private you"?

_____

_____

_____

_____

_____

_____

_____

_____

_____

_____

_____

_____

_____

_____

58. **What is your spirit animal and why?**

_____

_____

_____

_____

_____

_____

_____

_____

_____

_____

_____

_____

_____

_____

_____

59. If you could only have one tattoo, what would it be and why?

_____

_____

_____

_____

_____

_____

_____

_____

_____

_____

_____

_____

_____

_____

60. When do you feel the most courageous?

_____

_____

_____

_____

_____

_____

_____

_____

_____

_____

_____

_____

_____

_____

_____

61. **What's a tough decision you've made that you're proud of the outcome?**

_____

_____

_____

_____

_____

_____

_____

_____

_____

_____

_____

_____

_____

62. What's the most memorable negative experience from your childhood? How does it affect you today?

_____

_____

_____

_____

_____

_____

_____

_____

_____

_____

_____

_____

_____

_____

63. **What time of your life have you liked the most? Liked the least?**

_____

_____

_____

_____

_____

_____

_____

_____

_____

_____

_____

_____

_____

64. **If you were to receive an award, what would it be and why?**

_____

_____

_____

_____

_____

_____

_____

_____

_____

_____

_____

_____

_____

65. If a genie granted you three wishes, what would they be and why?

_____

_____

_____

_____

_____

_____

_____

_____

_____

_____

_____

_____

_____

66. Who in your life can you talk to about anything and everything?

_____

_____

_____

_____

_____

_____

_____

_____

_____

_____

_____

_____

_____

67. If you could live anywhere in the world, where would
it be and why?

_____

_____

_____

_____

_____

_____

_____

_____

_____

_____

_____

_____

_____

_____

68. **What do you wish more people knew about you?**

_____

_____

_____

_____

_____

_____

_____

_____

_____

_____

_____

_____

_____

_____

69. **What makes you different from most of the people you're surrounded by?**

_____

_____

_____

_____

_____

_____

_____

_____

_____

_____

_____

_____

_____

_____

70.   What do you love doing that most people avoid?

_____

_____

_____

_____

_____

_____

_____

_____

_____

_____

_____

_____

_____

_____

_____

71. Describe a dream you've had that you will never forget.

_____

_____

_____

_____

_____

_____

_____

_____

_____

_____

_____

_____

_____

_____

_____

72.   **What's your all-time favorite book and what did you learn from it?**

_____

_____

_____

_____

_____

_____

_____

_____

_____

_____

_____

_____

_____

73.   What habits are you proud of that you're consistent with?

_____

_____

_____

_____

_____

_____

_____

_____

_____

_____

_____

_____

_____

_____

74. What's a bad habit that you need to cut out of your life? What can you do today to take a step in the right direction?

_____

_____

_____

_____

_____

_____

_____

_____

_____

_____

_____

_____

_____

75.   In what ways has your personality changed over the years?

_____

_____

_____

_____

_____

_____

_____

_____

_____

_____

_____

_____

_____

_____

_____

76. **What do you believe is the purpose of your life?**

_____

_____

_____

_____

_____

_____

_____

_____

_____

_____

_____

_____

_____

_____

77. **What do you need to start doing differently to live a more honest and authentic life?**

_____

_____

_____

_____

_____

_____

_____

_____

_____

_____

_____

_____

_____

_____

Congratulations!

You've asked yourself tough questions and have gotten closer to figuring out who the fuck you are.

Following this page, I've added some bonus space for you to continue on your journey.

You can use it to reflect on what you learned from those 77 questions, to ask (and answer) yourself your own questions, to write when you're feeling overwhelmed or inspired, to use as a grocery list, to tear out and make paper airplanes, or anything in between.

If you'd like to share your thoughts with me, I'd love to hear from you. Email me at erikmyers1991@gmail.com

"Whenever you are about to find fault with someone, ask yourself the following question: What fault of mine most nearly resembles the one I am about to criticize?"

Marcus Aurelius

_____

_____

_____

_____

_____

_____

_____

_____

_____

_____

_____

_____

"Self-awareness gives you the capacity to learn from your mistakes as well as your successes. It enables you to keep growing."

Lawrence Bossidy

_____

_____

_____

_____

_____

_____

_____

_____

_____

_____

_____

_____

"The unexamined life is not worth living."

Socrates

_____

_____

_____

_____

_____

_____

_____

_____

_____

_____

_____

_____

_____

_____

"Humility is not about having a low self image or poor self esteem. Humility is about self-awareness."

Erwin McManus

_____

_____

_____

_____

_____

_____

_____

_____

_____

_____

_____

_____

_____

_____

"Wisdom tends to grow in proportion to one's awareness of one's ignorance."

Anthony de Mello

_____

_____

_____

_____

_____

_____

_____

_____

_____

_____

_____

_____

_____

_____

"In the light of calm and steady self-awareness, inner energies wake up and work miracles without any effort on your part."

Nisargadatta Maharaj

_____

_____

_____

_____

_____

_____

_____

_____

_____

_____

_____

_____

_____

"I think self-awareness is probably the most important thing towards being a champion."

Billie Jean King

"If your emotional abilities aren't in hand, if you don't have self-awareness, if you are not able to manage your distressing emotions, if you can't have empathy and have effective relationships, then no matter how smart you are, you are not going to get very far."

Daniel Goleman

_____

_____

_____

_____

_____

_____

_____

_____

_____

_____

_____

_____

"You can't get away from yourself by moving from one place to another."

Ernest Hemingway

_____

_____

_____

_____

_____

_____

_____

_____

_____

_____

_____

_____

_____

_____

"Everything that irritates us about others can lead us to an understanding of ourselves."

Carl Jung

_____

_____

_____

_____

_____

_____

_____

_____

_____

_____

_____

_____

_____

"Let us not look back in anger, nor forward in fear, but around in awareness."

James Thurber

_____

_____

_____

_____

_____

_____

_____

_____

_____

_____

_____

_____

_____

"The first step toward change is awareness. The second step is acceptance."

Nathaniel Branden

_____

_____

_____

_____

_____

_____

_____

_____

_____

_____

_____

_____

_____

"Every human has four endowments; self-awareness, conscience, independent will and creative imagination. These give us the ultimate human freedom. The power to choose, to respond, to change."

Stephen Covey

"What is necessary to change a person is to change his awareness of himself."

Abraham Maslow

_____

_____

_____

_____

_____

_____

_____

_____

_____

_____

_____

_____

_____

"Awareness allows us to get outside of our mind and observe it in action."

Dan Brule

_____

_____

_____

_____

_____

_____

_____

_____

_____

_____

_____

_____

"Awareness is like the sun. When it shines on things, they are transformed."

Thich Nhat Hanh

_____

_____

_____

_____

_____

_____

_____

_____

_____

_____

_____

_____

_____

_____

"Awareness is a key ingredient in success. If you have it, teach it, if you lack it, seek it."

Michael B. Kitson

_____

_____

_____

_____

_____

_____

_____

_____

_____

_____

_____

_____

_____

"Being self-aware is not the absence of mistakes, but the ability to learn and correct them."

Daniel Chidiac

_____

_____

_____

_____

_____

_____

_____

_____

_____

_____

_____

_____

_____

"Self-awareness is not self-centeredness, and spirituality is not narcissism. 'Know thyself' is not a narcissistic pursuit."

Marianne Williamson

_____

_____

_____

_____

_____

_____

_____

_____

_____

_____

_____

_____

_____

"Without self awareness we are as babies in the cradles."

Virginia Woolf

_____

_____

_____

_____

_____

_____

_____

_____

_____

_____

_____

_____

_____

_____

_____

"Self awareness is the ability to take an honest look at your life without any attachment to it being right or wrong, good or bad."

Debbie Ford

_____

_____

_____

_____

_____

_____

_____

_____

_____

_____

_____

_____

_____

"After all, all knowledge simply means self knowledge."

Bruce Lee

_____

_____

_____

_____

_____

_____

_____

_____

_____

_____

_____

_____

_____

_____

"When I discover who I am, I'll be free."

Ralph Ellison

_____

_____

_____

_____

_____

_____

_____

_____

_____

_____

_____

_____

_____

_____

"I have been and still am a seeker, but I have ceased to question stars and books; I have begun to listen to the teaching my blood whispers to me."

Hermann Hesse

_____

_____

_____

_____

_____

_____

_____

_____

_____

_____

_____

_____

_____

"Strong people have a strong sense of self-worth and self-awareness; they don't need the approval of others."

Roy T. Bennett

_____

_____

_____

_____

_____

_____

_____

_____

_____

_____

_____

_____

_____

"At the center of your being you have the answer; you know who you are and you know what you want."

Lao Tzu

_____

_____

_____

_____

_____

_____

_____

_____

_____

_____

_____

_____

"The curious paradox is that when I accept myself just as I am, then I can change."

Carl R. Rogers

_____

_____

_____

_____

_____

_____

_____

_____

_____

_____

_____

_____

"Find out who you are and do it on purpose."

Dolly Parton

_____

_____

_____

_____

_____

_____

_____

_____

_____

_____

_____

_____

_____

_____

"You don't need anybody to tell you who you are or what you are. You are what you are!"

John Lennon

_____

_____

_____

_____

_____

_____

_____

_____

_____

_____

_____

_____

_____

_____

"Anyone who knows me, should learn to know me again; For I am like the Moon, you will see me with new face everyday."

Rumi

_____

_____

_____

_____

_____

_____

_____

_____

_____

_____

_____

_____

_____

"Success comes from the inside out. In order to change what is on the outside, you must first change what is on the inside."

Idowu Koyenikan

_____

_____

_____

_____

_____

_____

_____

_____

_____

_____

_____

_____

_____

_____

"I know that I am intelligent, because I know that I know nothing."

Socrates

_____

_____

_____

_____

_____

_____

_____

_____

_____

_____

_____

_____

_____

"Be the best you can be."

Craig Myers

_____

_____

_____

_____

_____

_____

_____

_____

_____

_____

_____

_____

_____

Manufactured by Amazon.ca
Bolton, ON

32454369R00067